Since

Jesus

Came

to

My

House

Written and Illustrated by

P. R. Lee May

ISBN-13: 978-0-9846410-7-9
ISBN-10: 0-9846410-7-6

Originally printed in 1991
Second printing August 2013

Since Jesus Came to My House

God's Heartbeat LLC
9624 South Cicero #414
Oak Lawn, IL 60453
Email:
admin@Godsheartbeat-inc.com   or
godsheartbeat_inc@yahoo.com

Since Jesus Came to My House
by P. Lee May

God's Heartbeat LLC
Published in USA

Dedication

I dedicate this book to the Lord Jesus Christ (my Lord and savior), Father God, Holy Spirit, Jameta, Presita, Dolorita, and Juliet (my four blessings from God-our daughters); Dr. Asabi Yakini, Regina Lee, Camille Reid, Stephanie Adams, Cherlynn Jackson, John Reid III, Bishop Edward Peecher, and Minister Miriam.

They all encouraged me to step out in faith and do what God gave me to do.

TABLE OF CONTENTS

Introduction

Introduction

I woke up early one morning about 4 a.m. I could not get back to sleep. I began to think of all that had happened in my life. I thought about how far God had brought my family and I since Jesus came into my life. It has not been an easy journey but I have never nor am I ever alone.

There were times of no heat at home, no lights, and no food. When the heat ran out, I sought God and he made a change. When there were no lights, I prayed to God and He put the lights back on. Each time God came through miraculously for me.

I desired to work overtime one week to provide clothing for my children when they were younger. God said, "NO." I submitted to God in obedience. I did not work the overtime offered that week.

God sent by a woman from my job with a box and a few bags of designer clothing for all my girls. Though some items were used, they looked brand new. Moreover, other items were brand new with the price tags still on them!

When the food ran out, I prayed to God. My wonderful God sent relatives and friends by with bags of food. He is so awesome!

There was a time when we had no place to stay. I was married but separated from my husband and we have four daughters. So the girls and I had no place to live. For various reasons, we moved nine times in three years. God opened the doors each time. I grew more each time.

As I sat on my bed thinking of all that happened, I heard in the spirit what I had been hearing in service, at home, at work, and even when I laid down at night to sleep:

"Since Jesus came into my house to stay, things have not been the same!"

The anointing (the presence of God) was so heavy that I began to write what I heard the Spirit of God saying. I read it at church. But that was not enough. I needed to publish this writing.

"Lord, how?" I asked.

My precious Lord opened doors and sent other Christians to me. They showed me what the book should look like and how to put it together. My old pastor, Bishop Edward Peecher said,

> "God will never leave you without anything to work with or the materials in your home to provide for your family to do what He has called you to."

I knew what he was talking about. I had a typewriter at home. I knew how to type but I lacked the confidence that my typing was sufficient to complete any job for Jesus.

As I reflected on this, I realized that

my current job (a job I did not like) of data entering orders into the computer base at work for the past two years had built up my confidence enough to not only use a word processor but a typewriter ... any typewriter! It says in Romans 8:28,

> *"And we know that all things work together for the good to them that love God, to them who are called according to his purpose!"*

Hallelujah!

I started typing. Whenever I read this material to anyone or myself, I feel the precious anointing of Holy Spirit. I know that this will be a blessing to you and your family. Let God encourage you. Know that when you accept Jesus Christ into your life, you are never alone. God bless you!

Chapter One: The Guest

Since Jesus came
Into my heart,
Things have not been the same.
Just give me a few moments
And I'll explain.

I have a new love given directly from heaven above. I invited Jesus into my heart and there He now lives. I swept out the living room and shared that space. I rest at night and sleep like a baby since the Lord of my soul moved into my home.

I invited Him into the kitchen to be present at every meal. I opened up the bathroom to allow my soul to be cleansed. As I get before Him daily in prayer, He washes me clean. Sometimes my hair needs washing, so I can think clearly.

Sometimes my body needs soaking so the stink will go away. Jesus uses hyssop to present me spotless without blemish or wrinkle.

In my bedroom, He made sure all things not like Him were removed: the zodiac, wrong paintings, nude pictures, and worldly records. He even helped me clean my closets of clothes not like Him. He cares so much for me.

He took time to explain about women in pants, shorts, halters, and tight clothes. He helped me to purchase and He provided a new wardrobe.

When we walked into the children's room, Jesus began to throw out all of the old things that were no longer needed. He is our new landlord and there are certain things Jesus-Himself requires:

- prayer in the morning
- prayer at night
- obedience
- patience
- loving care
- training
- following instructions
- peace
- praise

- worship
- studying His word

There is so much to learn and so much to teach about Jesus.

We, Jesus and I, walked through the remainder of the house. This took some time for He showed me special ways of keeping my vessel clean. We stopped at some closets. There were some dead things that had to go! Some unclean things Jesus helped me to put out.

At first, it was hard to give up those things. I was used to them and in many cases, they were habits. But as I put my trust in Jesus, it became easier and easier to give those things up.

You know as I gave those things up, Jesus replaced them with things that edified Him. For example, where distress was evicted, Jesus gave **peace**. When we found hopelessness, we put it out and Jesus gave **hope**. It was the same with fear. Jesus replaced it with **trust**.

When we entered the dining room, Jesus gave me new eating habits. He gave me a special diet that I am to take as medicine every day. It is the Word of God. Jesus instructed me that **I must eat** the Word of God so that He could be strong inside of me. This Jesus explained would help me to stand in times of despair and testing.

As we were talking, someone knocked at the door. I ran without hesitation to the door. I left Jesus in the dining room. My old friends were there and I let them in. They seemed so relieved to be allowed in. They thought they could not come in again. Why there was:

- darkness
- questions
- doubt
- fear
- anxiety
- hopelessness
- depression

- worry
- defeat
- mistrust
- attitude
- unbelief
- confusion
- carelessness
- distraction
- unforgiveness
- hurt
- lying
- cheating
- rebellion
- selfishness

just to name a few.

They began flooding my house, messing up my new carpet, and destroying my soul. I began snapping at some people and not wanting to be around certain people. These old friends came in so quick that I forgot about prayer. They monopolized my time. And oh yes, self-pity was there.

I did not take my medicine. I did not read my Word of God. It got too hard to concentrate to pray. I was real weak.

Those old friends talked all day and complained all night. I began to find some of those old clothes and put them on. I even pulled out a few of those old records we boxed up to listen to them. Oh, how I wished I had not let them in.

Fear laughed because he gripped my soul! I didn't know what to do. I wanted the peace that Jesus had given me. And ... I ... I remembered Jesus. You know, as I said, "Jesus" I saw a little light. The darkness was not as great. I thought I saw a light coming from the bathroom. My old friends shouted,

> "Let's party some more! Don't go to that bathroom. That Jesus is not your friend. We stayed with you all these years through thick and thin. He just arrived. That Jesus will make you do things you

don't want to. He won't let you have any fun. He'll make you dead!"

As I began to cry, confusion took my hand. I didn't know what to do or what to say. Then the telephone rang. I answered it and distraction started messing with my children.

Anger welled up deep within me. But Jesus sent a new friend to talk with me. We prayed on the telephone.

Those old friends began to hide in my house. Some of them left completely when she shouted, "**THE BLOOD OF JESUS**, loose her and let her go!"

Confusion let go of my hand. Depression moved aside and he pulled pride. Defeat walked out of the door. Carelessness left too. Anger subsided and slowly crept out. Fear ran along with anger and he took doubt.

I began to say, "Yes, Lord. Yes, Lord."

Belief took control. Peace flooded my house. Joy walked in. I said, "Jesus," and darkness ran.

This new friend, this true friend talked so much about Jesus that I asked for forgiveness again and there He was in my presence. Why, He came out of the bathroom. He had been there waiting all the time for me! I told my new friend I had to go. Then Jesus took complete control.

We went into the bathroom. He washed my soul all over. Jesus used hyssop again. Then as we walked together through the rest of my home; He talked to me. Jesus showed me how to not only have peace within my soul but how to allow peace in each room of my house.

We anointed the walls with "a special oil." Then Jesus and I prayed to God. In Jesus' name, we requested peace. Then wouldn't you know it, some of those old friends were hiding under beds and in closets, especially in the children's room!

As God granted Peace to flood each room, Jesus explained these were no longer friends but now my enemies. I got angry and put them out! I opened the front door and told them not to come back, for at my home, they were welcomed no more!

Jesus helped me anoint the walls, the windows, and the doors. Then we asked God,

> "Father God allow the angels to protect us from hurt, harm and danger in Jesus' name, amen."

The air cleared. Quiet walked in. Angels filled my house and a few stood at my doors. I rested and I relaxed in peace.

Chapter Two: The Gift

When we entered the dining room, Jesus explained more principles to me. He emphasized the importance of my special diet. Jesus explained that fasting is concentration on and of Him. It allows for faith to increase and doubt to decrease.

He explained that fasting was abstinence from natural food; replaced by prayer, meditation, and absorbing the Word of God. Jesus also explained the urgency and need for fasting. It is needful to do spiritual warfare against our enemies as it gives strength to His angels warring on my behalf.

As I listened intently, there was a knock at the front door. This time I asked Jesus, "Should I answer the door?" I definitely did not want to experience what I had the last time.

Jesus walked with me to the front door. He smiled. I trembled all over. We opened the door together and in walked Holy Ghost! I had heard about him before. I wanted to know more about him. He is a celebrity in heaven you know. Now: Holy Ghost enters my house. I am overjoyed!

In the presence of Holy Ghost, I heard a new language. As I opened my mouth, my tongue moved and rolled. Then the new language came forth! Why it was not only different but refreshing.

There was a knot in my stomach. Tears streamed down my face. The knot unraveled and joy trickled through my soul. As the knot completely unfolded, I experienced unspeakable joy.

You see, Holy Ghost brought:

- strength
- keeping power
- reliance on Jesus

Besides this I received from Holy Spirit,

- a boldness to go forth

- an ability to talk about God to anyone
- a determination to tells others about Jesus

(Holy Spirit and Holy Ghost are the same.) Together Jesus, Father God, and Holy Spirit instruct me.

Like I said in the beginning, things are not the same since Jesus came to my house (in 1979). You see before I had periods of depression. Confusion and foolishness lead me around. I stayed spiritually blinded to what was happening in my life and the people around me.

My friends were wishy-washy with no foundation. I was unable to stand ground on issues I thought were right because "friends" easily influenced and dominated me. I allowed myself, many times to be put in trick bags and I paid the consequences.

But since Jesus came into my heart, I have been growing. The old

Presita left. She was evicted out of this body shell. A new Presita covered in the blood of Jesus entered in! The old Presita received encouragement from worldly records, people, gossip, lying, and deceiving people.

Why she would quickly agree, get angry at the drop of a hat: just that quick, and be ready to fight. The old Presita was ever seeking satisfaction somewhere. She felt unloved.

But the new Presita, my, my, my, I am different! I learned to depend daily on Jesus. For I know that without Jesus, I can do nothing! With Jesus,

> "*I can do all things through Christ which strengtheneth me,*" (Philippians 4:13 KJV).

I have a new Father. He's better than the old father. My new Father removed chains, destroyed yokes in my life, and brought me out of Egypt.

When I make mistakes, my new

Father is so sensitive to remember I am in a human body. **My new Father loves me**. And when I ask for forgiveness from my new Father for what I have done, He accepts me back and quickly restores me to my rightful place.

My old father would not have done that. As a matter of fact, my old father was a slave driver, who would heap more burdens, guilt, and shame on me!

Chapter Three: The Outcome

Yes! I have grown. Those enemies and more enemies have tried to deceive me and present themselves as friends. Those enemies attempted to steer me away from Jesus by telling me: He, Jesus, was wrong. Those enemies have tried to change my paths.

But thank God for Jesus, Father God, and precious Holy Spirit. Not only has Holy Ghost proved them wrong but Holy Ghost brought to my mind Jesus' word embedded deep within my soul so I could stand, not move, and hold ground. What I now believe in is: Jesus! What He says, I hold on to it.

Jesus said,

> *Know ye not that ye are the temple of God, and that the Spirit of God dwelleth in you? If any man (woman) defile the*

*temple of God, him shall
God destroy; for the temple of
God is holy, which temple ye
are (1 Corinthians 3:16-17
KJV).*

I no longer:

- smoke reefer (marijuana - joints)
- commit adultery
- drink wine
- curse
- lie
- steal
- cheat

Yes, I have been under reconstruction since 1979. I have had many re-fillings by Holy Ghost. My building was destroyed more than twice. But you see my house looked so much better when I first accepted Jesus Christ. The change was so great that I am now to the point that whatever happens I am going to stay with Jesus all the way to heaven!

At first, I did not run well. I stumbled, fell,

and broke my legs. At one point, I was not only undernourished but suffered from lunacy. But I have learned that:

> *God has not given us (me) the spirit of fear, but of power, and of love, and of a sound mind* (2 Timothy 1:7 KJV).

Not only am I different but I desire to stay with Jesus. I am going to stay with Jesus so I can be with Jesus in the end. Matthew 10:22 says

> *"And ye shall be hated of all men for my name's sake: but he that endureth to the end shall be saved."*

I now receive encouragement from:

- Father God
- Jesus
- Holy Ghost
- Jesus' Word
- fellowshipping with other saints of God
- from the pastor of my church

- from sermons
- in prayer
- in worship
- praising the Lord
- staying in the presence of God

Jesus is no longer just the landlord of my soul but I recently signed papers for Him to take permanent ownership and full possession. I know Jesus will never leave me.

I am not ever going to walk away from Jesus again. There is too much at stake. For He is a God that never, never fails! No I am not perfect but I know that Jesus loves me and is able to present me faultless before Father God without spot or wrinkle.

Jesus not only takes care of me but He does not even mind taking care of my four daughters. My inheritance with and through Jesus Christ is priceless! With the help and aid of Holy Ghost, I am able to:

- bear all things

- endure all things
- hope in all things
- believe all things

…and stand on Jesus, who is the Word of God. I have learned that if I cannot gain any ground then to at least hold the ground I possess.

By the way, those enemies I find have no power over me. For I learned that if God be for me, what, what is the world against me?

I take Jesus everywhere I go! I go with Jesus everywhere He desires me to go! There is so much to learn. Yes, I'm still learning day by day to be what Jesus desires me to be!

Other Books by the Author

Taking Authority Over Your Neighborhood
by P. Lee May

The book has 14 biblical principles that enable you to transform your own neighbor-hood to a tranquil atmosphere that is safe and secure no matter where you live.

Protecting Your Child in Prayer
by P. Lee May

This how-to-do book communicates specific prayer strategies for protecting your child from infant to adult.

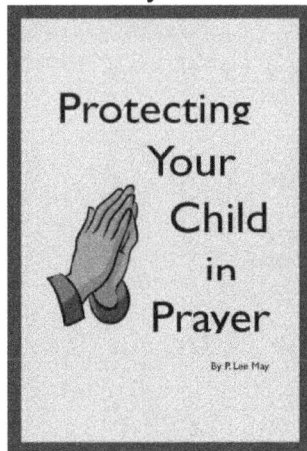

Laurie's Secret
by P. Lee May

Meet Laurie, Rosita, Trixie, Honey and Buck. The author's first children's book shares a family's mystery. Is Laurie the only one with a secret?

www.ingramcontent.com/pod-product-compliance
Lightning Source LLC
Chambersburg PA
CBHW030011040426
42337CB00012BA/735